D1621023

Miracles
of Jesus

NELSON/REGENCY

Nashville

�֍ �֍ ✤ ✤ ✤ ✤ ✤ ✤ ✤ ✤ ✤ ✤ ✤ ✤ ✤

Contents

�֍ �֍ �֍ ✷ ✷ ✷ ✷ ✷ ✷ ✷ ✷ ✷ ✷ ✷ ✷ ✷

Introduction

The miracles of Jesus retold here in their probable order of occurrence portray God's interest in every conceivable aspect of our lives. Whether the need involved was of eternal importance or simply the satisfying of the physical hunger of His tired followers, Jesus' compassion was evident. He met emotional needs when He completely freed a demoniac and also when He quieted a stormy sea and thus the fears of His disciples. He remedied financial problems and performed physical healings of great and small proportion. Even though many such stories are related in

❀ ❀ ❀ ❀ ❀ ❀ ❀ ❀ ❀ ❀ ❀ ❀ ❀ ❀

the Bible, the apostle John concluded
his book with these words:

> *And there are also many other
> things that Jesus did, which if
> they were written one by one, I
> suppose that even the world itself
> could not contain the books that
> would be written. Amen.*
>
> —John 21:25

Water
Becomes
Wine

✿✿✿✿✿✿✿✿✿✿✿✿✿✿✿✿✿

JOHN 2

1

On the third day there was a wedding in Cana of Galilee, and the mother of Jesus was there.

2

Now both Jesus and His disciples were invited to the wedding.

3

And when they ran out of wine, the

✿ ✿ ✿ ✿ ✿ ✿ ✿ ✿ ✿ ✿ ✿ ✿ ✿ ✿ ✿

*mother of Jesus said to Him, "They
have no wine."*

4

*Jesus said to her, "Woman, what
does your concern have to do with
Me? My hour has not yet come."*

5

*His mother said to the servants,
"Whatever He says to you, do it."*

6

Now there were set there six water-pots of stone, according to the manner of purification of the Jews, containing twenty or thirty gallons apiece.

7

Jesus said to them, "Fill the water-pots with water." And they filled them up to the brim.

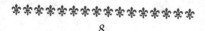

8

And He said to them, "Draw some out now, and take it to the master of the feast." And they took it.

9

When the master of the feast had tasted the water that was made wine, and did not know where it came from (but the servants who had drawn the water knew), the master of the feast called the bridegroom.

❊ ❊ ❊ ❊ ❊ ❊ ❊ ❊ ❊ ❊ ❊ ❊ ❊ ❊ ❊ ❊

10

And he said to him, "Every man at the beginning sets out the good wine, and when the guests have well drunk, then the inferior. You have kept the good wine until now!"

11

This beginning of signs Jesus did in Cana of Galilee, and manifested His glory; and His disciples believed in Him.

An Incredible
Catch of Fish

1

So it was, as the multitude pressed about Him to hear the word of God, that He stood by the Lake of Gennesaret,

2

and saw two boats standing by the lake; but the fishermen had gone from them and were washing their nets.

3

Then He got into one of the boats, which was Simon's, and asked him to put out a little from the land. And He sat down and taught the multitudes from the boat.

4

When He had stopped speaking, He said to Simon, "Launch out into the deep and let down your nets for a catch."

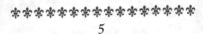

5

But Simon answered and said to Him, "Master, we have toiled all night and caught nothing; nevertheless at Your word I will let down the net."

6

And when they had done this, they caught a great number of fish, and their net was breaking.

7

So they signaled to their partners in the other boat to come and help them. And they came and filled both the boats, so that they began to sink.

8

When Simon Peter saw it, he fell down at Jesus' knees, saying, "Depart from me, for I am a sinful man, O Lord!"

✤ ✤ ✤ ✤ ✤ ✤ ✤ ✤ ✤ ✤ ✤ ✤ ✤ ✤ ✤

9

For he and all who were with him were astonished at the catch of fish which they had taken;

10

and so also were James and John, the sons of Zebedee, who were partners with Simon. And Jesus said to Simon, "Do not be afraid. From now on you will catch men."

11

So when they had brought their boats to land, they forsook all and followed Him.

Jesus Heals Peter's Mother-in-Law

MATTHEW 8

14

Now when Jesus had come into Peter's house, He saw his wife's mother lying sick with a fever.

15

So He touched her hand, and the fever left her. And she arose and served them.

Jesus Heals a Paralyzed Man

MARK 2

1

And again He entered Capernaum after some days, and it was heard that He was in the house.

2

Immediately many gathered together, so that there was no longer room to receive them, not even near the door. And He preached the word to them.

3

Then they came to Him, bringing a paralytic who was carried by four men.

4

And when they could not come near Him because of the crowd, they uncovered the roof where He was. So when they had broken through, they let down the bed on which the paralytic was lying.

5

When Jesus saw their faith, He said to the paralytic, "Son, your sins are forgiven you."

6

And some of the scribes were sitting there and reasoning in their hearts,

7

"Why does this Man speak blasphemies like this? Who can forgive sins but God alone?"

8

But immediately, when Jesus perceived in His spirit that they reasoned thus within themselves, He said to them, "Why do you reason about these things in your hearts?

9

"Which is easier, to say to the paralytic, 'Your sins are forgiven you,' or to say, 'Arise, take up your bed and walk'?

❊ ❊ ❊ ❊ ❊ ❊ ❊ ❊ ❊ ❊ ❊ ❊ ❊ ❊

10

*"But that you may know that the
Son of Man has power on earth to
forgive sins"—He said to the paralytic,*

11

*"I say to you, arise, take up your
bed, and go to your house."*

12

Immediately he arose, took up the

❊ ❊ ❊ ❊ ❊ ❊ ❊ ❊ ❊ ❊ ❊ ❊ ❊ ❊ ❊

bed, and went out in the presence of them all, so that all were amazed and glorified God, saying, "We never saw anything like this!"

Restoring a
Withered Hand

6

Now it happened on another Sabbath, also, that He entered the synagogue and taught. And a man was there whose right hand was withered.

7

So the scribes and Pharisees watched Him closely, whether He would heal on the Sabbath, that they might find an accusation against Him.

8

But He knew their thoughts, and said to the man who had the withered hand, "Arise and stand here." And he arose and stood.

9

Then Jesus said to them, "I will ask you one thing: Is it lawful on the Sabbath to do good or to do evil, to save life or to destroy?"

❀ ❀ ❀ ❀ ❀ ❀ ❀ ❀ ❀ ❀ ❀ ❀ ❀ ❀ ❀

10

And when He had looked around at them all, He said to the man, "Stretch out your hand." And he did so, and his hand was restored as whole as the other.

11

But they were filled with rage, and discussed with one another what they might do to Jesus.

Jesus Heals a Centurion's Servant

1

Now when He concluded all His sayings in the hearing of the people, He entered Capernaum.

2

And a certain centurion's servant, who was dear to him, was sick and ready to die.

3

So when he heard about Jesus, he

❀ ❀ ❀ ❀ ❀ ❀ ❀ ❀ ❀ ❀ ❀ ❀ ❀ ❀ ❀

sent elders of the Jews to Him, pleading with Him to come and heal his servant.

4

And when they came to Jesus, they begged Him earnestly, saying that the one for whom He should do this was deserving,

5

"for he loves our nation, and has built us a synagogue."

6

Then Jesus went with them. And when He was already not far from the house, the centurion sent friends to Him, saying to Him, "Lord, do not trouble Yourself, for I am not worthy that You should enter under my roof.

7

"Therefore I did not even think myself worthy to come to You. But say

❧ ❧ ❧ ❧ ❧ ❧ ❧ ❧ ❧ ❧ ❧ ❧ ❧ ❧ ❧ ❧

*the word, and my servant will be
healed.*

8

*"For I also am a man placed under
authority, having soldiers under me.
And I say to one, 'Go,' and he goes;
and to another, 'Come,' and he
comes; and to my servant, 'Do this,'
and he does it."*

9

When Jesus heard these things, He

❄ ❄ ❄ ❄ ❄ ❄ ❄ ❄ ❄ ❄ ❄ ❄ ❄ ❄

marveled at him, and turned around and said to the crowd that followed Him, "I say to you, I have not found such great faith, not even in Israel!"

10

And those who were sent, returning to the house, found the servant well who had been sick.

Widow's Son
Raised from
the Dead

11

Now it happened, the day after, that He went into a city called Nain; and many of His disciples went with Him, and a large crowd.

12

And when He came near the gate of the city, behold, a dead man was being carried out, the only son of his mother; and she was a widow. And

❀ ❀ ❀ ❀ ❀ ❀ ❀ ❀ ❀ ❀ ❀ ❀ ❀ ❀

a large crowd from the city was with her.

13

When the Lord saw her, He had compassion on her and said to her, "Do not weep."

14

Then He came and touched the open coffin, and those who carried him stood still. And He said, "Young man, I say to you, arise."

❈ ❈ ❈ ❈ ❈ ❈ ❈ ❈ ❈ ❈ ❈ ❈ ❈ ❈

15

So he who was dead sat up and began to speak. And He presented him to his mother.

16

Then fear came upon all, and they glorified God, saying, "A great prophet has risen up among us"; and, "God has visited His people."

Jesus Calms
a Storm

MARK 4

35

On the same day, when evening had come, He said to them, "Let us cross over to the other side."

36

Now when they had left the multitude, they took Him along in the boat as He was. And other little boats were also with Him.

37

And a great windstorm arose, and

❊ ❊ ❊ ❊ ❊ ❊ ❊ ❊ ❊ ❊ ❊ ❊ ❊ ❊ ❊

the waves beat into the boat, so that it was already filling.

38

But He was in the stern, asleep on a pillow. And they awoke Him and said to Him, "Teacher, do You not care that we are perishing?"

39

Then He arose and rebuked the wind, and said to the sea, "Peace, be

❀ ❀ ❀ ❀ ❀ ❀ ❀ ❀ ❀ ❀ ❀ ❀ ❀ ❀ ❀

still!'' And the wind ceased and there was a great calm.

40

But He said to them, "Why are you so fearful? How is it that you have no faith?"

41

And they feared exceedingly, and said to one another, "Who can this be, that even the wind and the sea obey Him!"

Jesus Heals a Demon-Possessed Man

✤ ✤ ✤ ✤ ✤ ✤ ✤ ✤ ✤ ✤ ✤ ✤ ✤ ✤ ✤

MARK 5

1

Then they came to the other side of the sea, to the country of the Gadarenes.

2

And when He had come out of the boat, immediately there met Him out of the tombs a man with an unclean spirit,

3

who had his dwelling among the

tombs; and no one could bind him, not even with chains,

4

because he had often been bound with shackles and chains. And the chains had been pulled apart by him, and the shackles broken in pieces; neither could anyone tame him.

5

And always, night and day, he was in the mountains and in the tombs, crying out and cutting himself with stones.

6

When he saw Jesus from afar, he ran and worshiped Him.

7

And he cried out with a loud voice and said, "What have I to do with You, Jesus, Son of the Most High God? I implore You by God that You do not torment me."

8

For He said to him, "Come out of the man, unclean spirit!"

9

Then He asked him, "What is your name?" And he answered, saying, "My name is Legion; for we are many."

10

Also he begged Him earnestly that He would not send them out of the country.

❖ ❖ ❖ ❖ ❖ ❖ ❖ ❖ ❖ ❖ ❖ ❖ ❖ ❖ ❖

11

Now a large herd of swine was feeding there near the mountains.

12

So all the demons begged Him, saying, "Send us to the swine, that we may enter them."

13

And at once Jesus gave them permission. Then the unclean spirits went out and entered the swine (there were

❄ ❄ ❄ ❄ ❄ ❄ ❄ ❄ ❄ ❄ ❄ ❄ ❄ ❄ ❄

about two thousand); and the herd ran violently down the steep place into the sea, and drowned in the sea.

14

So those who fed the swine fled, and they told it in the city and in the country. And they went out to see what it was that had happened.

15

Then they came to Jesus, and saw the one who had been demon-

❊ ❊ ❊ ❊ ❊ ❊ ❊ ❊ ❊ ❊ ❊ ❊ ❊ ❊ ❊ ❊

possessed and had the legion, sitting
and clothed and in his right mind.
And they were afraid.

16

And those who saw it told them
how it happened to him who had
been demon-possessed, and about the
swine.

17

Then they began to plead with Him
to depart from their region.

❀ ❀ ❀ ❀ ❀ ❀ ❀ ❀ ❀ ❀ ❀ ❀ ❀ ❀ ❀

18

And when He got into the boat, he who had been demon-possessed begged Him that he might be with Him.

19

However, Jesus did not permit him, but said to him, "Go home to your friends, and tell them what great things the Lord has done for you,

❧ ❧ ❧ ❧ ❧ ❧ ❧ ❧ ❧ ❧ ❧ ❧ ❧ ❧ ❧

and how He has had compassion on you."

20

And he departed and began to proclaim in Decapolis all that Jesus had done for him; and all marveled.

The Woman with the Hemorrhage Healed

MARK 5

25

Now a certain woman had a flow of blood for twelve years,

26

and had suffered many things from many physicians. She had spent all that she had and was no better, but rather grew worse.

27

When she heard about Jesus, she

❃ ❃ ❃ ❃ ❃ ❃ ❃ ❃ ❃ ❃ ❃ ❃ ❃ ❃ ❃

came behind Him in the crowd and
touched His garment.

28

For she said, "If only I may touch
His clothes, I shall be made well."

29

Immediately the fountain of her
blood was dried up, and she felt in
her body that she was healed of the
affliction.

✤ ✤ ✤ ✤ ✤ ✤ ✤ ✤ ✤ ✤ ✤ ✤ ✤ ✤ ✤

30

And Jesus, immediately knowing in Himself that power had gone out of Him, turned around in the crowd and said, "Who touched My clothes?"

31

But His disciples said to Him, "You see the multitude thronging You, and You say, 'Who touched Me?'"

32

And He looked around to see her who had done this thing.

33

But the woman, fearing and trembling, knowing what had happened to her, came and fell down before Him and told Him the whole truth.

❧ ❧ ❧ ❧ ❧ ❧ ❧ ❧ ❧ ❧ ❧ ❧ ❧ ❧ ❧

34

And He said to her, "Daughter, your faith has made you well. Go in peace, and be healed of your affliction."

The Feeding of the Five Thousand

MARK 6

30

Then the apostles gathered to Jesus and told Him all things, both what they had done and what they had taught.

31

And He said to them, "Come aside by yourselves to a deserted place and rest a while." For there were many coming and going, and they did not even have time to eat.

32

So they departed to a deserted place in the boat by themselves.

33

But the multitudes saw them departing, and many knew Him and ran there on foot from all the cities. They arrived before them and came together to Him.

34

And Jesus, when He came out, saw a

❊ ❊ ❊ ❊ ❊ ❊ ❊ ❊ ❊ ❊ ❊ ❊ ❊ ❊ ❊

great multitude and was moved with
compassion for them, because they
were like sheep not having a shep-
herd. So He began to teach them
many things.

35

When the day was now far spent,
His disciples came to Him and said,
"This is a deserted place, and already
the hour is late.

❋ ❋ ❋ ❋ ❋ ❋ ❋ ❋ ❋ ❋ ❋ ❋ ❋ ❋ ❋

36

"Send them away, that they may go
into the surrounding country and
villages and buy themselves bread;
for they have nothing to eat."

37

But He answered and said to them,
"You give them something to eat."
And they said to Him, "Shall we go
and buy two hundred denarii worth

❉ ❉ ❉ ❉ ❉ ❉ ❉ ❉ ❉ ❉ ❉ ❉ ❉ ❉ ❉ ❉

of bread and give them something to eat?''

38

But He said to them, "How many loaves do you have? Go and see." And when they found out they said, "Five, and two fish."

39

Then He commanded them to make them all sit down in groups on the green grass.

❀ ❀ ❀ ❀ ❀ ❀ ❀ ❀ ❀ ❀ ❀ ❀ ❀ ❀

40

So they sat down in ranks, in hundreds and in fifties.

41

And when He had taken the five loaves and the two fish, He looked up to heaven, blessed and broke the loaves, and gave them to His disciples to set before them; and the two fish He divided among them all.

❀ ❀ ❀ ❀ ❀ ❀ ❀ ❀ ❀ ❀ ❀ ❀ ❀ ❀ ❀

42

So they all ate and were filled.

43

And they took up twelve baskets full of fragments and of the fish.

44

Now those who had eaten the loaves were about five thousand men.

Jesus Walks on Water

22

Immediately Jesus made His disciples get into the boat and go before Him to the other side, while He sent the multitudes away.

23

And when He had sent the multitudes away, He went up on the mountain by Himself to pray. Now when evening came, He was alone there.

24

But the boat was now in the middle of the sea, tossed by the waves, for the wind was contrary.

25

Now in the fourth watch of the night Jesus went to them, walking on the sea.

26

And when the disciples saw Him walking on the sea, they were troubled, saying, "It is a ghost!" And they cried out for fear.

27

But immediately Jesus spoke to them, saying, "Be of good cheer! It is I; do not be afraid."

28

And Peter answered Him and said, "Lord, if it is You, command me to come to You on the water."

So He said, "Come." And when Peter had come down out of the boat, he walked on the water to go to Jesus.

30

But when he saw that the wind was boisterous, he was afraid; and beginning to sink he cried out, saying, "Lord, save me!"

❀ ❀ ❀ ❀ ❀ ❀ ❀ ❀ ❀ ❀ ❀ ❀ ❀ ❀ ❀

31

And immediately Jesus stretched out His hand and caught him, and said to him, "O you of little faith, why did you doubt?"

32

And when they got into the boat, the wind ceased.

33

Then those who were in the boat came and worshiped Him, saying, "Truly You are the Son of God."

A Syrophoenician's Daughter Is Healed

21

Then Jesus went out from there and departed to the region of Tyre and Sidon.

22

And behold, a woman of Canaan came from that region and cried out to Him, saying, "Have mercy on me, O Lord, Son of David! My daughter is severely demon-possessed."

❀ ❀ ❀ ❀ ❀ ❀ ❀ ❀ ❀ ❀ ❀ ❀ ❀ ❀ ❀

23

But He answered her not a word. And His disciples came and urged Him, saying, "Send her away, for she cries out after us."

24

But He answered and said, "I was not sent except to the lost sheep of the house of Israel."

❖ ❖ ❖ ❖ ❖ ❖ ❖ ❖ ❖ ❖ ❖ ❖ ❖ ❖ ❖

25

Then she came and worshiped Him, saying, "Lord, help me!"

26

But He answered and said, "It is not good to take the children's bread and throw it to the little dogs."

27

And she said, "Yes, Lord, yet even the little dogs eat the crumbs which fall from their masters' table."

❧ ❧ ❧ ❧ ❧ ❧ ❧ ❧ ❧ ❧ ❧ ❧ ❧ ❧ ❧

28

Then Jesus answered and said to her, "O woman, great is your faith! Let it be to you as you desire." And her daughter was healed from that very hour.

Taxes from a
Fish's Mouth

24

When they had come to Capernaum, those who received the temple tax came to Peter and said, "Does your Teacher not pay the temple tax?"

25

He said, "Yes." And when he had come into the house, Jesus anticipated him, saying, "What do you think, Simon? From whom do the

❧ ❧ ❧ ❧ ❧ ❧ ❧ ❧ ❧ ❧ ❧ ❧ ❧ ❧ ❧

kings of the earth take customs or taxes, from their sons or from strangers?''

26

Peter said to Him, ''From strangers.'' Jesus said to him, ''Then the sons are free.

27

''Nevertheless, lest we offend them, go to the sea, cast in a hook, and take the fish that comes up first. And

❊ ❊ ❊ ❊ ❊ ❊ ❊ ❊ ❊ ❊ ❊ ❊ ❊ ❊ ❊

when you have opened its mouth,
you will find a piece of money; take
that and give it to them for Me and
you.''

Jesus Raises Lazarus from the Dead

JOHN 11

1

Now a certain man was sick, Lazarus of Bethany, the town of Mary and her sister Martha.

2

It was that Mary who anointed the Lord with fragrant oil and wiped His feet with her hair, whose brother Lazarus was sick.

3

Therefore the sisters sent to Him, saying, "Lord, behold, he whom You love is sick."

4

When Jesus heard that, He said, "This sickness is not unto death, but for the glory of God, that the Son of God may be glorified through it."

5

Now Jesus loved Martha and her sister and Lazarus.

6

So, when He heard that he was sick, He stayed two more days in the place where He was.

7

Then after this He said to the disciples, "Let us go to Judea again."

8

The disciples said to Him, "Rabbi, lately the Jews sought to stone You, and are You going there again?"

9

Jesus answered, "Are there not twelve hours in the day? If anyone walks in the day, he does not stumble, because he sees the light of this world.

10

"But if one walks in the night, he

❊ ❊ ❊ ❊ ❊ ❊ ❊ ❊ ❊ ❊ ❊ ❊ ❊ ❊ ❊

stumbles, because the light is not in
him.''

11

These things He said, and after that
He said to them, "Our friend Lazarus sleeps, but I go that I may wake
him up.''

12

Then His disciples said, "Lord, if he
sleeps he will get well.''

❀ ❀ ❀ ❀ ❀ ❀ ❀ ❀ ❀ ❀ ❀ ❀ ❀ ❀

13

However, Jesus spoke of his death, but they thought that He was speaking about taking rest in sleep.

14

Then Jesus said to them plainly, "Lazarus is dead.

15

"And I am glad for your sakes that I was not there, that you may believe. Nevertheless let us go to him."

❉ ❉ ❉ ❉ ❉ ❉ ❉ ❉ ❉ ❉ ❉ ❉ ❉ ❉ ❉

16

Then Thomas, who is called the Twin, said to his fellow disciples, "Let us also go, that we may die with Him."

17

So when Jesus came, He found that he had already been in the tomb four days.

18

Now Bethany was near Jerusalem, about two miles away.

19

And many of the Jews had joined the women around Martha and Mary, to comfort them concerning their brother.

20

Then Martha, as soon as she heard that Jesus was coming, went and met Him, but Mary was sitting in the house.

21

Now Martha said to Jesus, "Lord, if

You had been here, my brother would not have died.

22

"But even now I know that whatever You ask of God, God will give You."

23

Jesus said to her, "Your brother will rise again."

24

Martha said to Him, "I know that

he will rise again in the resurrection at the last day."

25

Jesus said to her, "I am the resurrection and the life. He who believes in Me, though he may die, he shall live.

26

"And whoever lives and believes in Me shall never die. Do you believe this?"

❖ ❖ ❖ ❖ ❖ ❖ ❖ ❖ ❖ ❖ ❖ ❖ ❖ ❖ ❖

27

She said to Him, "Yes, Lord, I believe that You are the Christ, the Son of God, who is to come into the world."

28

And when she had said these things, she went her way and secretly called Mary her sister, saying, "The Teacher has come and is calling for you."

29

As soon as she heard that, she arose quickly and came to Him.

30

Now Jesus had not yet come into the town, but was in the place where Martha met Him.

31

Then the Jews who were with her in the house, and comforting her,

❄ ❄ ❄ ❄ ❄ ❄ ❄ ❄ ❄ ❄ ❄ ❄ ❄ ❄ ❄ ❄

when they saw that Mary rose up quickly and went out, followed her, saying, "She is going to the tomb to weep there."

32

Then, when Mary came where Jesus was, and saw Him, she fell down at His feet, saying to Him, "Lord, if You had been here, my brother would not have died."

❋ ❋ ❋ ❋ ❋ ❋ ❋ ❋ ❋ ❋ ❋ ❋ ❋ ❋ ❋

33

Therefore, when Jesus saw her weeping, and the Jews who came with her weeping, He groaned in the spirit and was troubled.

34

And He said, "Where have you laid him?" They said to Him, "Lord, come and see."

35

Jesus wept.

36

Then the Jews said, "See how He loved him!"

37

And some of them said, "Could not this Man, who opened the eyes of the blind, also have kept this man from dying?"

38

Then Jesus, again groaning in Him-

❊ ❊ ❊ ❊ ❊ ❊ ❊ ❊ ❊ ❊ ❊ ❊ ❊ ❊ ❊

self, came to the tomb. It was a cave,
and a stone lay against it.

39

Jesus said, "Take away the stone."
Martha, the sister of him who was
dead, said to Him, "Lord, by this
time there is a stench, for he has been
dead four days."

40

Jesus said to her, "Did I not say to

❋ ❋ ❋ ❋ ❋ ❋ ❋ ❋ ❋ ❋ ❋ ❋ ❋ ❋ ❋ ❋

you that if you would believe you would see the glory of God?"

41

Then they took away the stone from the place where the dead man was lying. And Jesus lifted up His eyes and said, "Father, I thank You that You have heard Me.

42

"And I know that You always hear

Me, but because of the people who are standing by I said this, that they may believe that You sent Me."

43

Now when He had said these things, He cried with a loud voice, "Lazarus, come forth!"

44

And he who had died came out bound hand and foot with grave-

❀ ❀ ❀ ❀ ❀ ❀ ❀ ❀ ❀ ❀ ❀ ❀ ❀ ❀ ❀

clothes, and his face was wrapped
with a cloth. Jesus said to them,
"Loose him, and let him go."

The Story of
Ten Lepers

12

As He entered a certain village, there met Him ten men who were lepers, who stood afar off.

13

And they lifted up their voices and said, "Jesus, Master, have mercy on us!"

14

So when He saw them, He said to them, "Go, show yourselves to the

✤ ✤ ✤ ✤ ✤ ✤ ✤ ✤ ✤ ✤ ✤ ✤ ✤ ✤ ✤

priests." And so it was that as they
went, they were cleansed.

15

And one of them, when he saw that
he was healed, returned, and with a
loud voice glorified God,

16

and fell down on his face at His feet,
giving Him thanks. And he was a
Samaritan.

❀ ❀ ❀ ❀ ❀ ❀ ❀ ❀ ❀ ❀ ❀ ❀ ❀ ❀ ❀ ❀

17

So Jesus answered and said, "Were there not ten cleansed? But where are the nine?

18

"Were there not any found who returned to give glory to God except this foreigner?"

19

And He said to him, "Arise, go your way. Your faith has made you well."

Bartimaeus
Receives
His Sight

46

Now they came to Jericho. As He went out of Jericho with His disciples and a great multitude, blind Bartimaeus, the son of Timaeus, sat by the road begging.

47

And when he heard that it was Jesus of Nazareth, he began to cry out and say, "Jesus, Son of David, have mercy on me!"

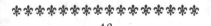

48

*Then many warned him to be quiet;
but he cried out all the more, "Son of
David, have mercy on me!"*

49

*So Jesus stood still and commanded
him to be called. Then they called
the blind man, saying to him, "Be of
good cheer. Rise, He is calling you."*

50

And throwing aside his garment, he rose and came to Jesus.

51

So Jesus answered and said to him, "What do you want Me to do for you?" The blind man said to Him, "Rabboni, that I may receive my sight."

Then Jesus said to him, "Go your way; your faith has made you well." And immediately he received his sight and followed Jesus on the road.

A Fig Tree Is Cursed and Withers

MARK 11

12

Now the next day, when they had come out from Bethany, He was hungry.

13

And seeing from afar a fig tree having leaves, He went to see if perhaps He would find something on it. When He came to it, He found nothing but leaves, for it was not the season for figs.

14

In response Jesus said to it, "Let no one eat fruit from you ever again." And His disciples heard it.

* * *

20

Now in the morning, as they passed by, they saw the fig tree dried up from the roots.

21

And Peter, remembering, said to

Him, "Rabbi, look! The fig tree which You cursed has withered away."

22

So Jesus answered and said to them, "Have faith in God.

23

"For assuredly, I say to you, whoever says to this mountain, 'Be removed and be cast into the sea,' and does not

❈ ❈ ❈ ❈ ❈ ❈ ❈ ❈ ❈ ❈ ❈ ❈ ❈ ❈ ❈

doubt in his heart, but believes that
those things he says will be done, he
will have whatever he says.

24

"Therefore I say to you, whatever
things you ask when you pray, believe that you receive them, and you
will have them."

Jesus Heals
Malchus's Ear

47

And while He was still speaking, behold, a multitude; and he who was called Judas, one of the twelve, went before them and drew near to Jesus to kiss Him.

48

But Jesus said to him, "Judas, are you betraying the Son of Man with a kiss?"

When those around Him saw what was going to happen, they said to Him, "Lord, shall we strike with the sword?"

50

And one of them struck the servant of the high priest and cut off his right ear.

But Jesus answered and said, "Permit even this." And He touched his ear and healed him.